Philip neri

Saint for Confirmation

1515-1595

Born in Florence, Italy

Feast Day: May 26

Patron saint of Rome, joy

U.S. Army Special Forces

Text by Barbara Yoffie
Illustrated by Jeff Albrecht

Liguori Publications
A Redemptorist Ministry

Dedication

To my family:
my parents Jim and Peg,
my husband Bill,
our son Sam and daughter-in-law Erin,
and our precious grandchildren
Ben, Lucas, and Andrew

To all the children I have had the privilege
of teaching throughout the years.

Imprimi Potest:
Stephen T. Rehrauer, CSsR, Provincial
Denver Province, the Redemptorists

Imprimatur:
In accordance with CIC 827, permission to publish has been granted on September 28, 2018, by the Most Reverend Mark S. Rivituso, Auxiliary Bishop, Archdiocese of St. Louis. Permission to publish is an indication that nothing contrary to Church teaching is contained in this work. It does not imply any endorsement of the opinions expressed in the publication; nor is any liability assumed by this permission.

Published by Liguori Publications, Liguori, Missouri 63057
To order, visit Liguori.org or call 800-325-9521.

ISBN 978-0-7648-2797-6

Liguori Publications, a nonprofit corporation, is an apostolate of the Redemptorists.
To learn more about the Redemptorists, visit Redemptorists.com.

Printed in the United States of America
22 21 20 19 18 / 5 4 3 2 1
First Edition

Dear Parents and Teachers:

Saints and Me! is a series of children's books about saints, with six books apiece in the first four sets. The first set, *Saints of North America,* honors holy men and women who blessed and served the land we call home. The second, *Saints of Christmas,* includes heavenly heroes who inspire us through Advent and Christmas and teach us to love the Infant Jesus. The third, *Saints for Families,* introduces saints who modeled God's love within and for the domestic Church. The fourth, *Saints for Communities,* explores individuals from different times and places who served Jesus through their various roles and professions.

The seven books in the *Saints for Sacraments* series explore eight saints who had great love for the sacraments. John the Baptist baptized Jesus in the Jordan River. Padre Pio helped people make a good confession. Teresa of Ávila was known for her great love of the Eucharist. Philip Neri received the Holy Spirit after praying to God. Louis and Zélie Martin, a married couple, taught their children to serve God and the poor. At an early age, John Vianney wanted to dedicate his life to God as a priest; today he is the patron saint of parish priests. Maximilian Kolbe battled poor health to become a priest and brought God's healing to sick people.

Name the saint who lived in the desert and ate locusts and honey. In this set of books, who was the saint with stigmata? Who began a Carmelite convent dedicated to prayer? Who grew up during the French Revolution? Which saints were the parents of Thérèse of Lisieux? Who volunteered to die in place of a stranger in a prison camp? Find out in the *Saints for Sacraments* set—part of the *Saints and Me!* series—and help children connect to the lives of the saints.

Introduce your children or students to the *Saints and Me!* series as they:

—**READ** about the lives of the saints and are inspired by their stories.

—**PRAY** to the saints for their intercession.

—**CELEBRATE** the saints and relate them to their lives.

Saints for Sacraments

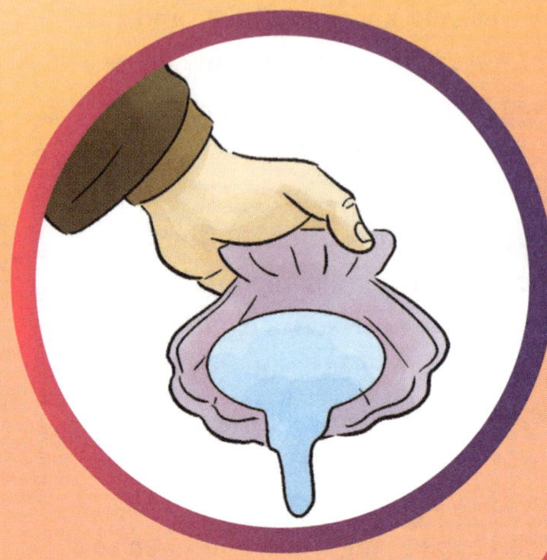

John the Baptist
Baptism

Teresa of Ávila
Eucharist

Philip Neri
Confirmation

Padre Pio
Reconciliation

Maximilian Kolbe
Anointing of the Sick

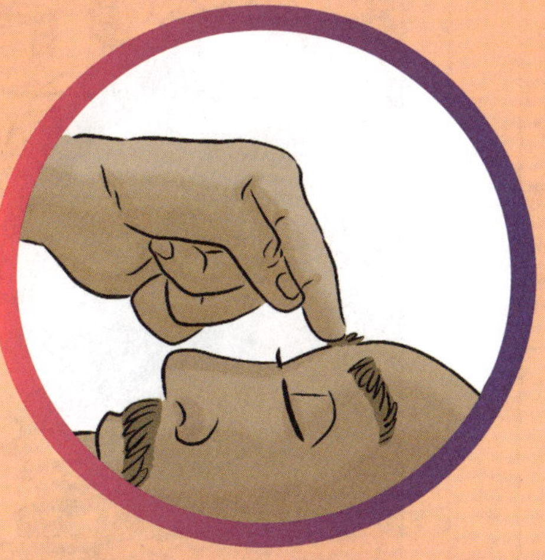

Louis and Zélie Martin
Matrimony

John Vianney
Holy Orders

Philip Neri, an Italian priest, is called the "saint of joy." God blessed him with many special gifts. Philip used the gifts of the Holy Spirit to help people in the city of Rome grow in their faith. In the sacrament of confirmation, we also receive the gifts of the Holy Spirit. These special gifts help us follow Jesus and lead a holy life.

Philip was born in 1515 in Florence, Italy, and grew up in a happy and loving home. He was a good student and popular with other children. He was a natural leader. Philip was funny and kind to everyone. He was such a cheerful little boy that people called him "good little Philip."

When he was eighteen, Philip went to live with an uncle in a nearby city. His uncle was a successful businessman. "Philip, I will teach you everything I know. One day you will be rich like me," he promised. Philip smiled. He was not sure he wanted to be a rich businessman.

Philip liked to spend his time praying. He loved quiet time with God. He prayed to Mary. And he prayed to the Holy Spirit. “Holy Spirit, please help me to love God with all my heart.” After a short time, Philip felt God calling him to the city of Rome. Here he would do God’s work. Philip thanked his uncle and set out on his journey.

Rome was a large city with big problems. Many people had forgotten about their faith. It was not important to them anymore. Some priests did not care about helping people. Philip's faith was strong and he wanted to help, but how? He decided to enter the university, where he studied very hard and learned many new things.

A few years later he gave up his studies to spend more time working among the people in Rome. During the day Philip walked around the city talking to everyone about the good news of Jesus. At night he prayed. Philip prayed in old churches and in the catacombs, where the first Christians are buried. He felt close to God in these holy places.

One night, while praying in the catacombs, something amazing happened! Philip prayed, "Holy Spirit, give me your special gifts. Fill my heart with your love." Suddenly Philip saw a ball of fire. The fire entered his mouth and moved into his heart! He felt very warm and fell to the ground. Philip was filled with God's love and the joy of the Holy Spirit!

At baptism we receive the gifts of the Holy Spirit for the first time. When we are older, the Holy Spirit comes to us again in the sacrament of confirmation. Now we are ready to understand how to use the gifts of the Holy Spirit. The gifts strengthen us and help us to act more like Jesus. We grow in knowledge, understanding, courage, and reverence. These gifts help us learn good habits such as love, peace, patience, kindness, and joy.

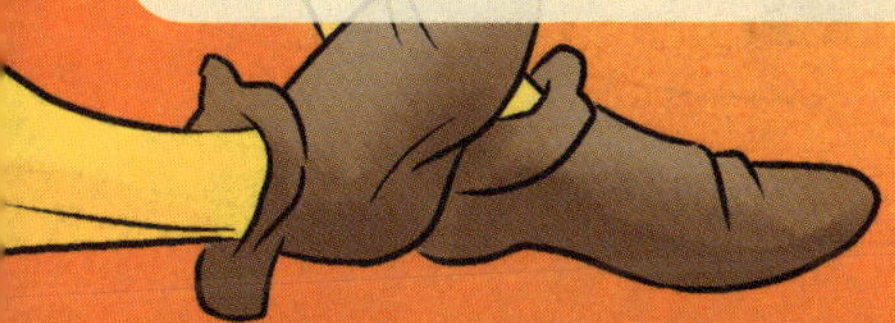

Philip shared his gift of joy with everyone he met. People loved to talk and joke with him. Philip's kind words led others to do kind actions. "When should we do some good?" he asked a group of young men. "How about right now?" Philip laughed and said, "Follow me!" He led them to a hospital where they spent the morning cleaning rooms. Later they fed the sick and prayed with them.

Philip organized more groups to help the poor and homeless in the city. There was so much work to do! "Philip, your work is holy and good! Why not do more and serve God as a priest?" asked his friend. Philip decided that God was calling him to the priesthood. Ordained at age thirty-six, he was excited to begin his new duties.

Father Philip Neri loved to celebrate Mass. The Eucharist was the center of his life. He wanted people to come to Mass often. "Come meet Jesus. He loves you!" Father Philip Neri spent several hours each day hearing confessions, guiding and bringing people back to God. They felt the joy of God's forgiveness in their hearts.

In the afternoon, a small group of men met in Father Philip Neri's room to pray, read Scripture, and talk about their faith. Before long, this small group grew into a large group called the Congregation of the Oratory, with Father Philip Neri as its holy leader.

He knew special ways to lead the faithful to God. Crowds gathered to hear talks about the saints and Church history. Singing and prayer were very important, too. Fun trips to different churches included picnics and more singing! "We should always be in good spirits," he said.

Father Philip Neri served God with a cheerful heart. He brought the people in the city of Rome back to the faith and helped them to be happy and holy. The Holy Spirit worked through Philip to do God's work so the Church could grow. We can pray to the Holy Spirit every day for special gifts. By sharing our gifts we can joyfully lead others to God just like Father Philip Neri!

Be full of joy, be full of fun!
Share your faith with everyone.

Saint Philip Neri,
The Holy Spirit filled you
with special gifts.
You were kind, happy,
and full of joy!
You led people to Jesus.
Help me share
the joy of my faith
with others.
Amen.

GLOSSARY (New Words)

Baptism: The sacrament that makes us children of God and members of the Church

Catacombs: An underground cemetery; some early Christians and martyrs are buried here

Congregation of the Oratory: A community of priests and lay brothers founded by Saint Philip Neri in 1575

Confirmation: The sacrament that seals us with the gifts of the Holy Spirit that we received at baptism

Eucharist: The sacrament in which bread and wine become the Body and Blood of Jesus

Holy Spirit: The third person of the Blessed Trinity

Ordination: To receive the sacrament of holy orders and become a deacon, priest, or bishop

Reverence: The gift of the Holy Spirit that helps us to show respect for God

Rome: A large city in Italy where Vatican City is located

Sacraments: Seven special signs of God's life and love